AF423505

THIS SERIES IS DEDICATED TO ALL THE YOUNG GIRLS THAT

BELIEVE THEY DO NOT HAVE A PLACE IN STEM.

KNOW THAT YOU ARE MORE THAN WORTHY,

DO NOT LET ANY ISSUES/BARRIERS GET IN YOUR WAY.

YOU CAN DO IT!

TO ALL MY BLACK AND BROWN GIRLS, KNOW THAT YOU

HAVE A PLACE IN THE STEM FIELD.

THE TIME IS NOW TO KICK THE DOOR WIDE OPEN AND

SHOW THE WORLD YOU HAVE EARNED THE RIGHT

TO BE EXACTLY THERE.

GET READY TO SHOW UP AND SHOW OUT!

KEEP YOUR HEAD HELD HIGH AND LET'S GET TO WORK!

WE
ARE
TRAVELLING
TO
EGYPT
EGYPT

Piper was a curious and adventurous little puppy who loved to explore the world around her and discover new things. Her favorite companion on her adventures was her big sister, Tabia. Tabia was a kind and patient girl who shared Piper's love of discovery. She was always happy to take her little sister on her travels, and together they visited many different countries and experienced many different cultures.

One day, Tabia decided to take Piper on a special trip to Egypt. She had always been fascinated by the ancient pyramids and wanted to share this wonder with her sister.

As they exited the airport in Egypt, the hot desert air hit their faces, and Piper felt excitement wash over her. She had never been to a place like this before and couldn't wait to explore everything Egypt had to offer.

AIRPORT

On the other hand, Tabia had been to Egypt before, but she still felt a sense of awe as she gazed at the beautiful scenery. They were both amazed by the vast desert landscapes and the towering pyramids in the distance.

"Look at those palm trees, Piper," she said, pointing to the trees swaying in the warm breeze. "They're so tall and majestic, aren't they?"

Piper wagged her tail and barked in agreement.

"Woof! Woof!! They're beautiful, sis!" she said, looking up at the palm trees with wonder.

As they drove towards the pyramids, they passed by colorful marketplaces, where vendors sold everything from spices and souvenirs to beautiful handmade rugs. Piper was fascinated by the bright colors and smells of the markets, and she kept poking her nose out of the car window to take it all in.

TAXI

When they finally arrived at the pyramids, Piper was struck by their sheer size. She couldn't believe people had built these massive structures many years ago.

Tabia noticed Piper's amazement and smiled. "Can you believe that the pyramids were built over 4,000 years ago, Piper?" she said as they walked towards the base of the pyramids. "It's amazing what people can accomplish with hard work and determination."

Piper nodded in agreement, still staring at the towering structures. She was in awe of the precision and engineering required to build the pyramids.

Tabia continued, "Did you know that the ancient Egyptians used math to help them build the pyramids? They used geometry to measure the land and determine the angles needed for the pyramid's shape."

Piper's ears perked up in interest, and she tilted her head. "Really? Math helped them build the pyramids?" she said, surprised. Tabia nodded, "Yes! And not just math but science and engineering too. The Egyptians used science to study the movement of the sun and stars and engineering to figure out how to move the heavy stone blocks and construct the pyramids."

NOD
NOD

Piper couldn't believe how much she was learning on this trip. "That's amazing, Tabia! I never knew that math and science could be used to build such incredible structures."

Tabia smiled, "Exactly! That's why STEM fields are so important, Piper. They allow us to create and innovate in ways we never thought possible. Who knows, maybe one day you'll use math and science to build something as amazing as the pyramids!"

Piper's tail wagged excitedly at the thought. "Woof! Woof!! That would be so cool, Tabia!" she said.

WOOF!!
WOOF!!

As they walked around the pyramids, Piper couldn't help but see everything in a new light. The intricate carvings and hieroglyphics on the walls suddenly seemed more meaningful, knowing they were created using math and science.

After admiring the pyramids, Tabia told Piper, "Let's go check out the Nile river, too, while we're here. To get to the Nile River, Tabia asked some locales for directions. When they finally got to the river, they were amazed by the sheer size of the body of water. The river stretched for miles, and they could see other people around it.

As they walked along the banks of the Nile River, Tabia pointed out the fields and farms that dotted the landscape.

"The Nile River was the lifeblood of ancient Egypt, Piper," she said. "It provided water for crops and allowed people to travel and trade."

Piper tilted her head, curious. "How did they know when to plant their crops?" she asked. Tabia smiled, "That's where astronomy comes in. The ancient Egyptians used the stars to determine the changing of the seasons.

They knew that when certain stars appeared in the sky, it was time to start planting or harvesting."

Piper's eyes widened in amazement.

"Wow, I had no idea the stars could be used for that," she said.

Tabia nodded, "And they used science and engineering to create innovative irrigation systems that allowed them to grow crops in the desert. They built canals and levees to control the river's flow and direct water to the fields."

Piper looked around at the lush green fields and the winding river, and she felt a new found appreciation for the ingenuity of the ancient Egyptians.

As they continued their exploration of Egypt, Piper and Tabia learned more about the importance of STEM fields in ancient times. They saw how math and science were used to construct incredible monuments and buildings and how astronomy and engineering played vital roles in everyday life.

By the end of their trip, Piper felt inspired to learn more about these fields. "Tabia, I want to learn more about STEM," she said. "I want to understand how we can use these fields to create a better world."

"We'll learn how to use our knowledge to make the world a better place together," Tabia replied.

It was finally time to go. The sisters had gotten to check out some fantastic tourist attractions, and they had learned so much about Egypt's rich culture and history. As they prepared to head back home, Piper couldn't help but feel grateful for the amazing adventure she had shared with her sister. "I had so much fun, Tabia," Piper said as they sat in the airport waiting for their flight. "Thank you for bringing me on this amazing trip.

Coffee

Tabia smiled and ruffled Piper's fur. "I'm glad you enjoyed it, Piper," she said. "I always love sharing my travels with you."

Piper looked out the window at the beautiful sunset over the desert, feeling a sense of peace and contentment. She knew she would never forget her trip to Egypt and looked forward to all the adventures ahead for her and Tabia.